# UGLY

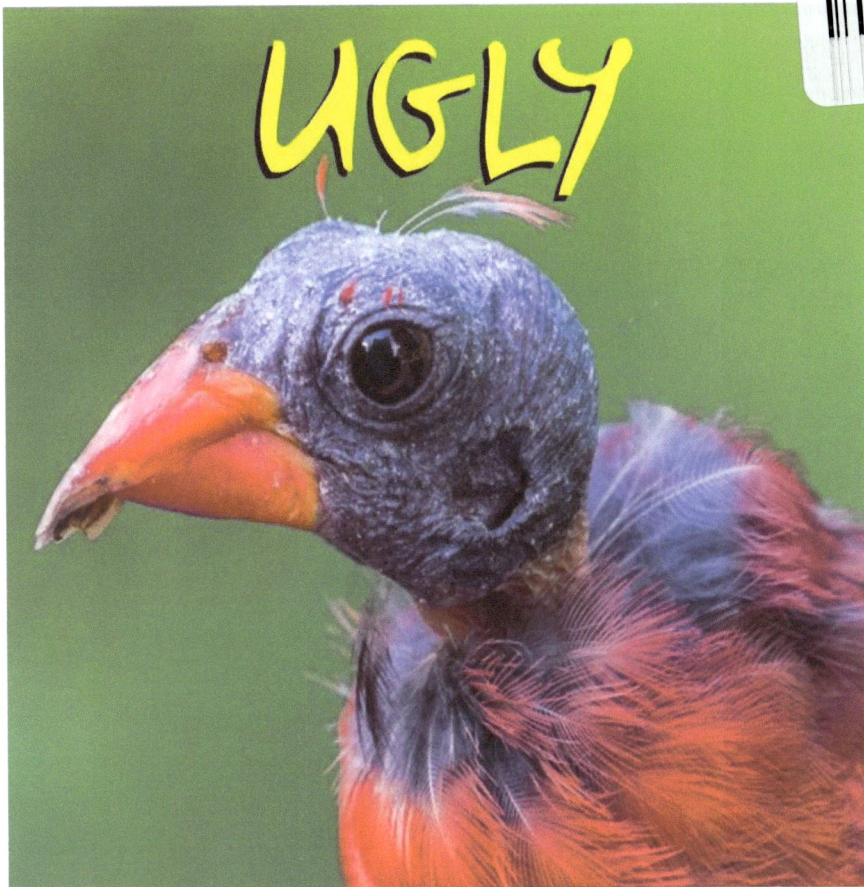

Written by Normandy D. Piccolo
Photos by Jim Sutherland

Normandy's Bright Ideas
Florida

Proceeds from 'Ugly' are donated to:
The Wild Bird Fund
565 Columbus Avenue
New York, NY 10024
www.wildbirdfund.org


Educators and librarians, please visit us at www.NormandysBrightIdeas.com
Photo Credits: Jim Sutherland
Written by: Normandy D. Piccolo


UGLY

Printed in the United States of Americas
Copyright ©2016 by Normandy's Bright Ideas
ISBN: 978-0985932992

First Edition
~
10  9  8  7  6  5  4  3  2

*"But they that wait upon the LORD shall renew their strength;*
*they shall mount up with wings as eagles;*
*they shall run, and not be weary;*
*and they shall walk, and not faint."*
**– Isaiah 40:31**

# A Seed of History

U.S. FISH & WILDLIFE SERVICE HEADQUARTERS
5275 LEESBURG PIKE, MS: MB
FALLS CHURCH, VA 22041-3803
Phone# (703)358-1714 or 1784
FAX# (703)358-2272 or 2282

The Northern Cardinal specie was a popular caged bird in the 1800's due to their bright red plumage and beautiful song. But, in 1918, the "Migratory Bird Treaty Act" was passed, making it illegal to capture, kill, possess, buy, sell, trade, ship, import, or export a migratory bird including feathers, parts, nests, or eggs, except under the terms of a valid permit issued pursuant to Federal regulations. The treaty was first created between the United States and Great Britain, and later signed by Mexico, Japan and the former Soviet Union. Cardinals are considered a protected migratory bird.

My name is "El Feo", which in Spanish means, "The Ugly One". I am a Northern Cardinal and I am supposed to look like this.

# DID YOU KNOW?

The Northern Cardinal is also known as: Cardinalis cardinalis, the Virginia Nightingale and the Red bird.

The Northern Cardinal is so named for the red plumage of the male, which happens to resemble the red vestments of a Cardinal in the Catholic Church.

The average lifespan of the Northern Cardinal is 3-9 years. During a banding study, a female Cardinal in Pennsylvania was documented as having lived 15 years and 9 months.

The Northern Cardinal is a medium-sized bird that is 7–9 inches tall and is the only documented red bird with a crest, in the United States.

Male Cardinals have bright red feathers. Female Cardinals feathers appear in various shades of grey and brown, with duller hits of red located on the tail, crest and wings.

Both male and female Cardinals have bright orange/red colored beaks and long tails. They are characterized by a unique crest on top of their heads.

The male Cardinal has a black mask which extends down to his chest. The female Cardinal has dark markings on her face, but no mask.

Northern Cardinals are related to: Grosbeaks, Sparrows and Finches.

Instead, I look like this: bald, with a few sporadic feathers sticking up in different places on my head and a broken beak. But, I did not always appear this way. Nobody knows for sure why this happened to me, but there are a few theories.

3

# DID YOU KNOW?

Baldhead Syndrome happens when a Cardinal loses all of its head and neck feathers at the same time. Blue Jays get this, too. Shedding old feathers to grow new ones is known as a "molt". During a typical molt, feathers drop off of the bird sporadically, not simultaneously.

The Cardinal molts in the late summer and early fall in order to prepare for winter. The new feathers grow back within several weeks, unless the bird has Baldhead Syndrome. Then, regrowth may take longer or not happen at all.

Ornithologists, specialists that study the physical appearance, flight and migration patterns and song of birds have differing opinions on the cause of Baldheaded Syndrome.

a: The birds are young and going through their first prebasic molt, prior to growing their winter feathers.

b: A simultaneous molt—when the bird loses almost all feathers rapidly. Mites, lice, the environment and/or nutrition can be factors causing this situation. Sometimes growths or scabby looking skin can be present. Northern Cardinals have black skin. Presence of another color could indicate a disease affecting the bird. Regrowth of feathers is usually in a staggered format.

c: Head injury. Birds can be hit by cars or fly into windows.

Back when I was a young juvenile, I made a visit to Mr. Jim's backyard and I have been visiting him almost daily, ever since. We have been "distant" friends for almost three years now. As you can see, back then, I had a full set of feathers on my head and a normal looking beak.

5

# DID YOU KNOW?

Young Cardinals (Juveniles) resemble female Cardinals and have black or grey colored beaks, instead of the traditional bright orange/red beak. As the young bird grows, the beak will change from black to cream, before becoming a permanent orange/red color.

Juvenile Cardinals are known to follow their parents on the ground for several days after leaving the nest. During this stage, they are called "fledglings".

A fledgling is a bird that flies down from the nest, but can't yet fly up into a tree. The birds can flutter their wings, but are unable to gain flight. This is considered a normal stage in growth and development. During this time, fledglings are often mistaken as being ill or injured when they are not.

Mom and Dad are up in the trees or in low lying shrubs nearby keeping an eye on them during this time and protecting them from predators. Also, the bright red colors of the male change to a duller brown, like his mate, in order to help disguise him and further protect his family.

The young Cardinals remain with their parents until they are able to forage for food on their own.

I grew into quite a handsome male, even though my feathers may not have been as brightly colored red as the other Northern Cardinals around me. The brightness of my feathers has to do with my diet. Foods like grapes and dogwood berries help birds like me maintain a bright red hue. Without those foods, my feathers turn dull and I appear disheveled.

# DID YOU KNOW?

Northern Cardinals do not migrate. They are known to stay within a few miles of where they were hatched.

The Northern Cardinal is recognized as the official state bird in 7 states: Ohio, West Virginia, Virginia, North Carolina, Kentucky, Illinois and Indiana.

Northern Cardinals can be found in: Canada, Hawaii, mainland U. S. and throughout Mexico. Some species of Cardinals have also been found in South America.

Northern Cardinals adapt well to parks and suburban human habitats. This accounts in part for their widespread presence.

Northern Cardinals are considered to be vain, feisty little creatures. They are aggressive with protecting their territory, especially during mating season. They have been spotted attacking their own reflection in a mirror or window, sometimes for hours at a time. The crest on a Northern Cardinal is raised when the bird is feeling emotional and flattened upon its head when feeling calm.

The Northern Cardinal does not sleep much and is known to sing before sunrise.

Every Summer I am supposed to molt. My feathers naturally and sporadically drop off and I grow new ones in their place to help prepare me for the upcoming winter season. But, something weird happened in my case. I molted and lost all of my feathers at once. Normally my head is covered again within a few weeks, but my feathers still have not completely grown back in and no one knows why this happened.

9

# DID YOU KNOW?

Northern Cardinals get their red feathers from eating certain foods like grapes and dogwood berries.

The red color comes from carotenoids in their food. Carotenoids are fat-soluble pigments that give color to the feathers.

During digestion certain red pigments from foods, like grapes or dogwood berries, enter into the bird's bloodstream and travel into the feather follicles where they then crystallize.

If a Northern Cardinal is unable to eat red pigmented foods, their bright red hue begins to fade.

I began feeling lonely in the month of March, and knew it was time for me to find a wife and have a family. I am a "one female for life" kind of bird, so this particular mate was going to have to be someone very special. She was going to have to be the kind of female who dug partially bald males like me. It should not be too hard to find her. Look at me. I am irresistible.

# DID YOU KNOW?

The mating season for the Northern Cardinal begins in the spring time, particularly during the month of March.

In order to choose an ideal mate, the male Cardinal first releases calls of anger and aggressively chases other male suitors away from his intended target.

After a good fight, the male Cardinal will then perch himself high on a tree top and sing a beautiful song to the female.

The brighter red in color the feathers are on the male Cardinal, the more his chances of finding a successful mate are increased.

The male Cardinal performs what is known as "mate-feeding", where during courtship, he feeds the female. This often gives the illusion that the two birds are kissing.

During mate-feeding, the Cardinal makes a "took" sound when preparing to feed their mate. Both male and female birds make this sound.

Mate-feeding continues until the female Cardinal lays all of her eggs and then proceeds to sit on them until they hatch. The egg laying produces a "clutch".

The Northern Cardinal produces up to 3 clutches a year in the southern states and 1 clutch in the Northern states.

Wow! Isn't the girl of my dreams a knock-out? She is what a grown adult female Cardinal should look like. She is considered to be the ideal mate for me. To impress her, I have to perch on top of a tree and sing her a beautiful song. She is supposed to be attracted to my bright feathers, too. The brighter red my feathers are, the better my odds are of winning her heart. But there are two problems with the mating ritual. One, I cannot sing. And two, my feathers are very dull. I wound up losing her heart to a full plumaged, bright red, colored male with Pavarotti lungs. I was sad, but not ready to give up. I would find my girl...eventually.

# DID YOU KNOW?

The Northern Cardinal is monogamous and mates for life.

Northern Cardinals gather in flocks during the winter months. The flocks have been known to have between 60 – 70 birds at one time.

During the following spring, when mating season begins, birds within the flock pair off and separate from the group.

Meet my wife, Bella, which in Spanish means "Beautiful". The moment we bumped into one another inside of a hedge, I knew she was the one for me. I could not wait to impress her with my quirky personality. Remember, I cannot sing and my feathers are rather dull. Oh, and I'm bald. But, so is Bella. We were a perfect match and before long, I won her over with my mate-feeding skills. Turns out, Bella is a big fan of grasshoppers. Before long, we joined together and built our little "love nest". Actually Bella built it, but I helped by bringing her some of the necessary nesting materials.

15

# DID YOU KNOW?

Male Cardinals will fight wrens, catbirds, crows and sparrows for a nesting site.

Both male and female Cardinals scout out possible locations to build a nest. This process can take up to 2 weeks.

Northern Cardinals never use the same nest twice.

A nest takes 3–9 days to build. The final nest is cup-shaped, 2-3 inches tall, 4 inches across with a 3 inch inside diameter.

A Northern Cardinal nest has four layers and is made of: dry leaves, twigs, dry grass, grape vines, pine needles, strips of bark, various trash items and roots. It is then lined with leaves, grass and sometimes hair.

Cardinal nests are usually built in: bushes, low trees, near city gardens, in fields, thickets, near houses, by a water source, in parks, bushy swamps and sometimes on the edge of a forest.

A female Cardinal will lay between 2-5 eggs per clutch. The eggs are bluish/beige in color with light brown/olive colored spots.

The female Cardinal will lay eggs within a week of completing the nest. She will not sit on the nest until all of her eggs have been laid. The incubation period is usually 11-13 days.

The male Cardinal cares for the female Cardinal during this time by bringing her food while she is sitting on the eggs.

And baby makes three. Meet our baby, "Isabel".

# DID YOU KNOW?

When a baby Cardinal first comes out of an egg, it is called a hatchling or a chick.

Young birds are called fledglings, hatchlings or nestlings.

Baby Cardinals have to be fed frequently because what goes in, comes out pretty quick, and therefore leads to hunger. The babies are fed approximately every fifteen minutes.

What goes in-must come out- and does so in a fecal sac. Fecal sacs from the babies are gathered up by the tending parent and discarded at a site far from the nest or sometimes ingested by the parents. The purpose of this activity is to help protect the babies from predators and keep the nest clean.

Sometimes older baby birds will back their butts up to the edge of the nest and poop over the side. The poop then lands on the ground below.

Isn't that the most beautiful baby you have ever seen in your life? I say "that" instead of "him or her" because Isabel is still in the juvenile stage. Until the feathers begin to molt and change color, we will not know if Isabel is really a male or female. For now, we are assuming it's a girl.

.Mr. Jim was able to capture pictures of me feeding Isabel while we were out on one of our adventures. While I am still feeding Isabel, I am also teaching Isabel how to search for food.

As you can see, I am a very devoted father.
Isabel is wearing me out with that appetite I am trying to satisfy!
The kid is a bottomless pit for food!

# DID YOU KNOW?

Baby birds need a very rich protein based diet in order to grow and develop properly. Baby Cardinals open their mouths wide, indicating they want to be fed. This behavior prompts mom and dad to go hunting for food.

Newly hatched Cardinals are fed insects and worms by both of their parents. Some types of insects fed to hatchlings are: beetles, grasshoppers, termites, larvae, flies and cicadas.

Northern Cardinal parents tend to ingest smaller sized insects for themselves and bring the larger ones back to the nest to feed to their brood.

Parent birds kill insects by smashing them against an object or the ground. This helps to soften up the hard, exterior shell of the insect making it easier for the baby bird to ingest it.

All insects are fed to the babies intact. They have very large mouths and are quite capable of swallowing giant bugs.

So, a peculiar thing began happening to my beak as I grew older. I developed what is known as a "Malocclusion". My upper beak grows long over to the side of my lower beak. I am still able to eat like a champ. I somehow manage to trim the beak myself by pecking something hard like a tree trunk or thick branch, either deliberately or when killing an insect to eat myself, or to feed Isabel. Mr. Jim has different pictures of me where you can see my beak has been shortened here and there.

# DID YOU KNOW?

Bird beaks are made of bone and keratin. Keratin continually grows in beaks, like hair and fingernails do on humans.

Malocclusion occurs when the upper and lower parts of a bird's beak do not line up. Malocclusion can be caused by injury, poor nutrition (such as a lack of Vitamin A) or a genetic abnormality.

Malocclusion beaks can hinder a bird's ability to eat and drink properly. This can result in illness, extreme weight loss and eventual death for the bird if not corrected.

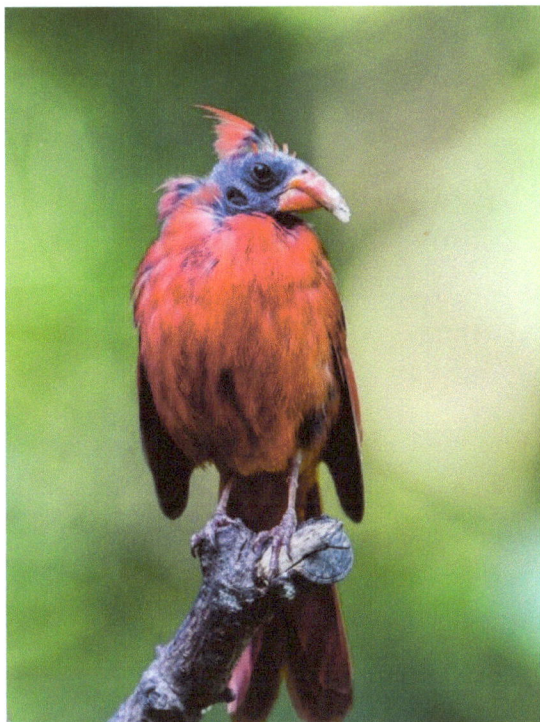

One of my favorite pastimes is to sit on a branch and admire the beautiful nature around me. Of course, I'm always keeping an eye out for a tasty insect to nibble on. Normally I would sing a song, but as I told you before, I cannot sing. I am not sure if it is because of my malocclusion beak, or maybe because I cannot carry a tune. I am quite the oddball. But a loveable one — just ask my wife, Bella. I hope I spot a grasshopper soon. Remember, those are Bella's favorite food. I won her heart by feeding her one during "mate-feeding".

25

# DID YOU KNOW?

Both male and female Northern Cardinals sing year around. The peak of singing season for the Northern Cardinal is in the spring and early summer. Female Cardinals sing more frequently than the male Cardinals and have a more complex melody to their song.

Northern Cardinals can have up to a total of 16 different songs in their repertoire.

Female Cardinals will sing while sitting on a nest of eggs to alert the male Cardinal to bring something to eat.

Bonded male and female Cardinals share bits of song back and forth to one another. This is considered to be a form of communication between the pair of birds. The female Cardinal sings actual notes to the male during communication, while the male Cardinal will often make a "clink" sound in return.

I am always on the lookout for predators, especially when I am on the ground searching for my favorite beauty product — Ants. Ants help keep what feathers I do have shiny during a molt, and also free of lice. And, they are quite a tasty snack in between placement, too. A three-tiered ant always hits the spot. Gulp! Burp! Oh, excuse me.

# DID YOU KNOW?

The Northern Cardinal has many predators including: owls, hawks, foxes, cowbirds, raccoons, skunks, opossums, and cats.

"Anting" is practiced by over 200 species of birds, including the Northern Cardinal. Those who have studied birds are unsure as to why this particular activity occurs, but some suggest it has something to do with molting or as a means to prevent lice.

"Anting" is performed in two ways. The bird will strategically place live ants into their plumage. Or, the bird will mash the ants and then smear their carcasses on their bodies.

When I pay a visit to Mr. Jim, I always let him know I have arrived by making a loud "tink" sound. It is the only sound he has ever heard me make. I have been known to "tink" up to six times in one day. I do this because I am hungry. I am quite the little piggy. Mr. Jim always has my favorite food ready to eat when I make an appearance.. Safflower seeds. Sometimes he mixes in some fresh grapes,too. Yum!

# DID YOU KNOW?

The Northern Cardinal makes the following sounds:

A "Took" sound is made when feeding one another during mate-feeding.

A "Chip" sound is an alarm call alerting that there is danger in the area. The sound is intended to scare a predator away. The sound is also made when females approach the nest, when carrying food to the nest, and when attempting to get nestlings to leave the nest.

A "Clink" sound is made when communicating with one another. This sound is made by the male Cardinals.

A "Tink" sound is "El Feo's" signature sound to Mr. Jim. No one can confirm if he makes this sound with his wife, Bella, or if he makes any other sounds. So far, "tink" is the only confirmed sound heard coming from him.

Due to bullies on the main bird feeder, mostly nasty blue jays, Mr. Jim decided to build me my own special bird feeder. He hangs it down low, close to the back door so I can access it easier. One time I was so hungry I landed on the feeder before Mr. Jim had a chance to finish hanging it up. He is usually quick with the service, but sometimes…?

31

# DID YOU KNOW?

Cardinals are considered to be "Omnivore" meaning they eat foods of plant and animal origin. They typically forage for food at dawn and dusk.

The Northern Cardinal's diet consists of: grasses, weed seeds, sap, small berries, grapes, grain, sunflower seeds, safflower seeds, nuts, fruit and insects.

The Cardinal ingests insects such as: 51 types of beetles, 4 types of grasshoppers, termites, ants, dragonflies, flies, 12 types of homopteras like aphids, cicadas, and leaf hoppers.

The Northern Cardinal's beak is strong enough to crack open seeds. They help vegetation growth by dispersing seeds.

Cardinals drink by scooping water into their beak and then tilting their head back. Bathing is done in streams, ponds and birdbaths.

The Northern Cardinal is a favorite visitor to backyard feeders and birdhouses.

Mr. Jim keeps my special feeder protected by hiding it inside of this black storage container until I show up and "tink", letting him know I am hungry.

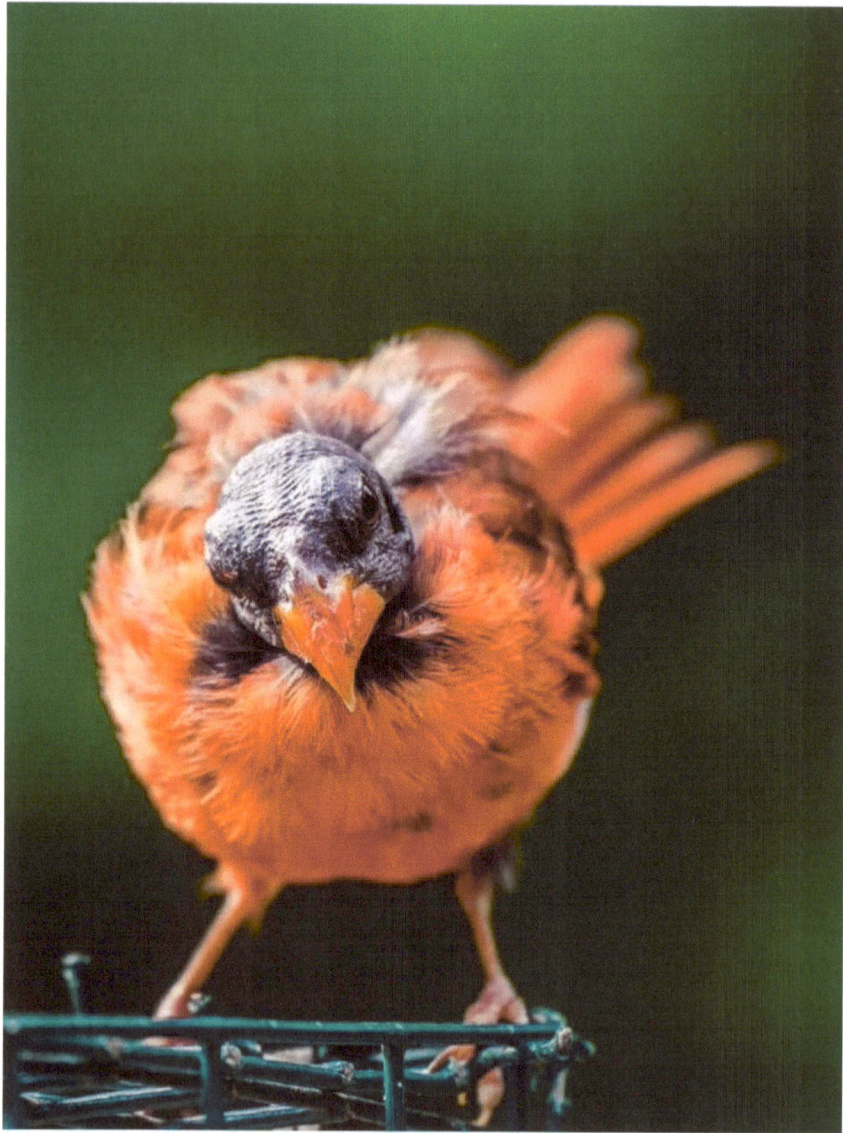

"Tink! Tink! Tink! Where are you Mr. Jim? I'm starving."

Sometimes Mr. Jim will make a "click" sound and I fly down to greet him.

One time, Mr. Jim recorded my "tink" sound and played it back to me on his phone. I freaked out and flew away. But, once my tummy started growling for those delicious Safflower seeds, I returned.

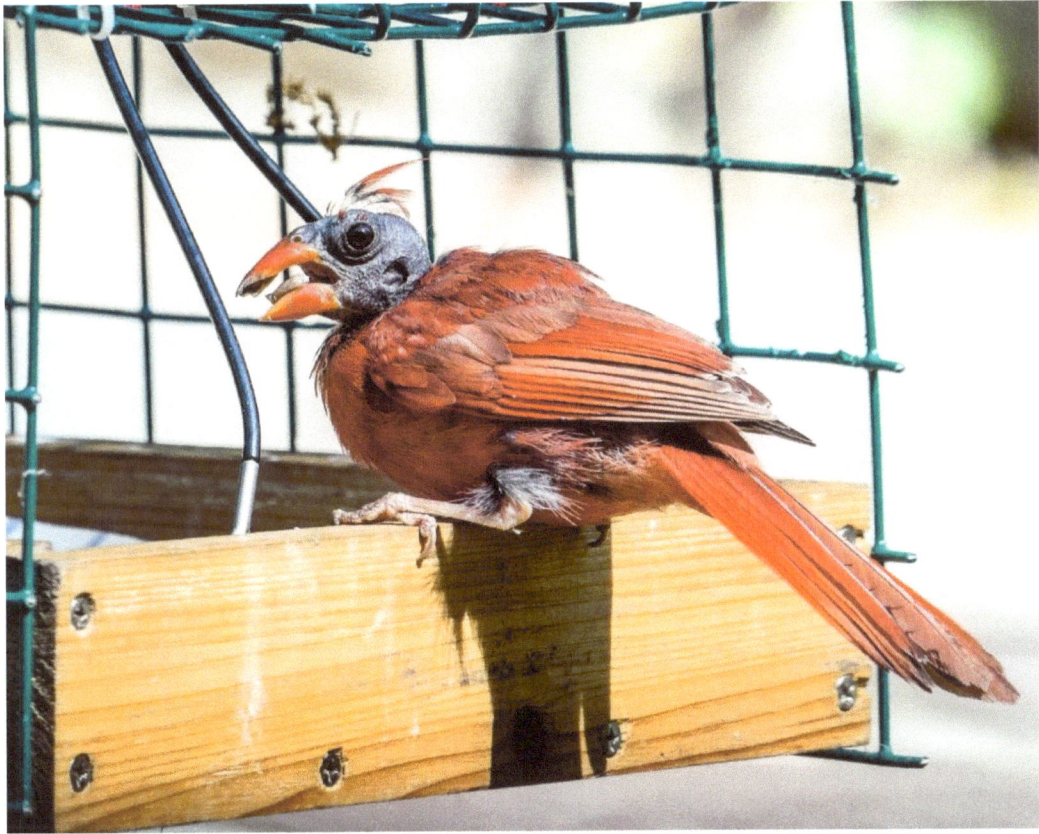

Mr. Jim says I can be silly sometimes by not being able to find the entrance to my special feeder right away. I will climb all around the feeder trying to poke through the bars at the seeds. I can't help it. My tummy over-rules my brain and I suppose I get foggy-headed. I do manage to figure it out...eventually and eat until I'm almost ready to pop. Yummy! Safflower seeds!!

Here I am eating a Safflower seed. Once I saw a catbird drop a grape, so I swooped down and picked it up. After that, Mr. Jim started adding grapes to my feeder. Mr. Jim spoils me so much. He must really love me.

My beak got too long, so I smashed it up against something and gave it a good trim.   My beak appears tattered, but it works.  I am still able to crack open sunflower seeds and eat.  Although, I think I might need to go to cosmetology school and learn how to give myself a more fashionable beak cut next time.

39

Here is an older picture of me, back when I had more feathers on my head, eating a sunflower seed. Some things never change. Well, except for the balding thing. But, bald is beautiful. Right?

Mr. Jim is so sneaky. He caught me mimicking a robin a few years ago. The robin had grabbed a juicy pink earthworm out of the ground, so I decided to give it a try, myself. I was a young, curious birdy back in the day. The worm may have wiggled and squiggled, but I fought it and eventually gobbled it down.

Here is my friend, "Gatita", a catbird, taking a sunbath. It is not uncommon to see Cardinals, like me, hanging around different birds such as; Wrens, Catbirds, Crows and English Sparrows. I can be friendly, except during mating season.

Gatita looked like she was having so much fun that I decided to take a sunbath nearby and soak up some Vitamin D, too. I just hope I don't burn my little bald birdy chrome dome in the process.

43

Here is Daddy's little girl, Isabel, all grown up. She follows me now everywhere I go. As you can see, Isabel has my eyes and Bella's perfect beak. I just hope Mr. Jim has enough Safflower seeds to feed both of us. Isabel inherited my hearty appetite, too.

I realize that I do not look like your average, everyday Northern Cardinal, and I accept that fact. I am who I am. My appearance and malocclusion beak have not stopped me from living a full birdy life.

I may still be bald at this time, but I am happy, loved and well cared for by Mr. Jim and his family, and my wife, Bella. I am so thankful Mr. Jim hears my "tinks" and looks out for me.

I am currently being monitored by Mr. Jim who is in contact with a wild life facility about me. Should any issues arise and it becomes apparent I can no longer eat, fly, hunt or drink on my own, immediate action will be taken and I will get help. For now, I appear to be thriving just fine. I am a free bird.

Thank You for reading my story and for helping wildlife with the purchase of this book.

THE END

48

# Common Backyard Bird Diseases

(Stock Photograph)

# Questions, Discussions & Activities

49

# Common Backyard Bird Diseases

House Finch Disease (Mycoplasmal Conjunctivitis): Eyes are red, swollen, runny or crusty. Transmission can occur when flocking, particularly at bird feeders. Some birds recover. Some die of starvation, exposure or predators.

Avian Pox: (Phase 1) Wart like growths appears on the featherless areas of the bird's body; around the eye, base of the beak, the legs and the feet. (Phase 2) The plague forms on the mucous membranes of the mouth, throat, trachea and lungs. The bird's breathing and feeding ability is impaired. This disease is spread by direct contact with an infected bird or contaminated feeder, or by eating contaminated food and water.

Aspergillosis: Fungal infection which affects the respiratory system. Symptoms of this disease include; difficulty breathing, emaciation, and increased thirst and trouble walking. The eyes will display white opacity and discharge. The disease is spread by ingesting or inhaling mold spores from contaminated food.

Salmonellosis: Common illness in feeder birds. Symptoms of this disease include; a thin body, fluffed up feathers, depressed, pasted vents and swollen eyelids, lethargic and easy to approach due to weakness. The disease is spread by fecal contamination of food and water by sick birds.

Trichomoniasis: A disease pigeons, doves and birds of prey who feed on them are affected by the most. The symptoms of this disease include; raised lesions in the mouth, esophagus and crop. Sick birds can contaminate birdbaths with oral secretions and expose other birds to the disease.

**If you find a sick bird report it to a state or local wildlife agency or to a wildlife rehabilitator in your area.**

For additional information about bird diseases please contact:

USGS National Wildlife Health Center
6006 Schroeder Road
Madison, WI 53711-6223
(608) 270-2400
www.nwhc.usgs.gov

USGS – NWHC Honolulu Field Station
P.O. Box 50187
300 Ala Moana Blvd.
Honolulu, HI 96850, USA
(808)792-9520

# Questions

1. What is El Feo's favorite food to eat?


2. Name five predators of the Northern Cardinal.


3. True or False
   The female Cardinal is red.


4. What three sounds do Cardinals make?


5. What year was the Migratory Bird Treaty Act passed?


6. What five countries signed the Migratory Bird Treaty Act?


7. What is the purpose of the Migratory Bird Treaty Act?

8. What is the name of the condition which causes El Feo's feathers to fall out?


9. True or False
   Adult Cardinals feed their babies seeds only.


10. What types of materials do Cardinals use to build a nest?


11. Who bullied El Feo on the bird feeder?


12. What is the sound that El Feo makes to get Mr. Jim's attention?


13. What is the sound that Mr. Jim makes to get El Feo's attention?


14. Name the two types of birds that Mr. Jim caught El Feo mimicking.


15. Name the five most common types of Backyard Bird Diseases.

16. What month does mating season begin for the Northern Cardinal?

17. What are the six causes of Baldheaded Syndrome?

18. True or False
    A flock of Cardinals can contain up to 70 birds.

19. What is the name of El Feo's mate? What does her name mean?

20. What is mate-feeding?

21. Name seven foods a Northern Cardinal eats.

22. True of False
    Cardinals help vegetation growth by dispersing seeds.

23. Does a Northern Cardinal mate for life?

24. True of False
    Mr. Jim built El Feo his own special feeder.


25. What is it called when a Cardinal smears live or dead ants on its feathers?


26. Why does a Cardinal smear live or dead ants on its feathers?


27. How many eggs does a female Cardinal lay in one clutch?


28. How many clutches of eggs a year does a female Cardinal lay?


29. How many layers are there in a Cardinal nest?


30. Circle the type of beak does El Feo has:
    Hooked Beak
    Normal Beak
    Scissors Beak
    Malocclusion Beak
    Crooked Beak

# Discussions & Activities

1. Discuss what causes a male Cardinal to fight its own reflection in a window or mirror for hours.

2. Create a shoebox diorama or a poster of a habitat where El Feo and his wife, Bella would live.

3. Create a nest like El Feo and Bella's using the same materials they do.

4. Create a timeline of El Feo's life.

5. List and then discuss what makes El Feo different from other Northern Cardinal Birds.

6. Discuss the differences between the male and female Cardinals; their appearance, mate-feeding, building the nest, hunting for food, and caring for the babies.

7. Discuss what you would do if you were to find an injured wild bird.

8. Discuss what you learned about the Northern Cardinal that you did not know before.

9. Discuss how you might relate to El Feo. Do you feel different or like an outcast?

10. Do you accept yourself like El Feo accepts himself? If so, why do you accept yourself. If not, why? What would you change?

11. Discuss the ailment that Blue Jays and Cardinals have in common. Are there other things these two types of birds have in common? If so, what are those things? Discuss how the two types of birds are different.

12. Create a timeline of events in El Feo's life. What was the most important event that happened in El Feo's life? Why do you think that particular event was more important than the others?

13. Discuss what you would do if you were to find a sick or injured wildlife bird.

14. Hang a bird feeder in your backyard and watch birds show up to eat the seeds. Write down what birds you see.

15. Make your own bird feeder from scratch. There are many fun and easy designs available online to choose from: Toilet Paper Roll Bird Feeders, Plastic Lids, Pinecone Bird Feeders, Orange Shell Bird Feeders and more.

# What to Feed

(Stock Photograph)

# Wild Birds

Black-oil sunflower seeds attract cardinals, chickadees, finches, blue jays and sparrows.

Fruits such as orange slices, grapes, raisins, pumpkin seeds, apple seeds attract mockingbirds, robins, bluebirds, catbirds, orioles and waxwings.

Hulled sunflower seeds are a favorite of cardinals, chickadees, blue jays, finches and sparrows.

Peanuts, whether in the shell or not, are a favorite of blue jays, titmice, chickadees and nuthatches.

Safflower seeds are consumed mostly by cardinals and blue jays.

Oats are a favorite of doves and quail.

Remember to keep a small dish of water handy for birds to drink, if you do not have a bird bath in your yard. Please make sure to change the water daily in order to prevent infection and the spread of disease.

*DO NOT FEED WILDLIFE/WILDBIRDS JUNKFOOD OF ANY KIND.*

# Name the Food & Then Circle "Yes or No"
## If It Can Be Fed To Wild birds

_____
Yes or No

_____
Yes or No

_____
Yes or No

_____
Yes or No

_____
Yes or No

_____
Yes or No

_____
**Yes or No**

_____
**Yes or No**

_____
**Yes or No**

_____
**Yes or No**

_____
**Yes or No**

_____
**Yes or No**

Yes or No

Yes or No

Yes or No

Yes or No

Yes or No

Yes or No

_____
**Yes or No**

_____
**Yes or No**

_____
**Yes or No**

# The Answers

1.  Safflower Seeds
2. Owls, Foxes, Cats, Raccoons, Skunks, Hawks, Cowbirds and Opossums
3. False
4. Clink, Chip & Took
5. 1918
6. United States, Great Britain, Mexico, Japan and the former Soviet Union
7. To protect wildlife birds from being captured, killed, possessed, bought, sold, traded, shipped, imported or exported
8. Baldheaded Syndrome
9. False
10. Dry leaves, twigs, dry grass, grapevines, pine needles, strips of bark, various trash items, roots
11. Blue Jays
12. Tink
13. Click
14. Catbird and Robin
15. House Finch Disease, Avian Pox, Aspergillosis, Salmonellosis and Trichomoniasis.
16. March
17. Prebasic molt, lice, mites, simultaneous molt, environment/nutrition and head injury
18. True
19. Bella and Beautiful
20. Where the male feeds the female during courtship
21. Grasses, weed seeds, sap, small berries, grapes, grain, sunflower seeds, safflower seeds, fruits, nuts and insects.
22. True
23. Yes
24. True
25. Anting
26. Molting and lice prevention

27. 2-5 eggs per clutch
28. 3 clutches per year (on average)
29. 4
30. Malocclusion beak


## Name the Food Answers: (Across)

Peanuts – Yes
Donut – No
Grapes – Yes
Cookies – No
Water – Yes
Sunflower Seeds – Yes
Orange Slices – Yes
Oats – Yes
Raisins – Yes
Soda – No
Pumpkin Seeds – Yes
Chocolate – No
Safflower Seeds – Yes
Potato Chips – No
Cherries – Yes
Apples – Yes
Pecans – Yes
Mealworms – Yes
Acorns – Yes
Almonds – Yes
Walnuts - Yes

www.ingramcontent.com/pod-product-compliance
Lightning Source LLC
Chambersburg PA
CBHW060822270326
41931CB00002B/48